The Night Sky

Written by Phillip Clarke
Designed by
Nayera Everall, Marc Maynard
& Candice Whatmore
Illustrated by John Woodcock

Contents

The Moon

PLATO (crater)

ARCHIMEDES
(crater)

SEA OF
SERENITY

APPENINE
MOUNTAINS

SEA OF
CRISES

OCEAN
OF STORMS

SEA OF
TRANQUILITY

COPERNICUS (crater)

● Where people first
landed on the Moon

SEA OF
CLOUDS

SEA OF
NECTAR

GRIMALDI
(crater)

TYCHO
(crater)

The Moon is bare and rocky, full of craters and holes.
You can see its larger features with the naked eye.
The dark patches on its surface are known as 'seas',
but are really flat areas of liquid rock that hardened
billions of years ago. The Moon has mountains, too,
but you'll need binoculars or a telescope to see them.

Moon phases

The Moon reflects light from the Sun. As it orbits the Earth, you see varying amounts of its sunlit side.

New moon
The Moon passes between the Sun and the Earth and is hard to see.

Waxing crescent
As the Moon moves out of line with the Sun, a sunlit crescent waxes (grows).

First quarter
A quarter of its way around the Earth, half the Moon's face is visible.

Waxing gibbous
Waxing from half- to fully lit

Full moon
Halfway around the Earth, the Moon's face is fully lit by the Sun.

Waning gibbous
It wanes (shrinks) as it falls into shadow.

Last quarter
Three-quarters of its way around the Earth

Waning crescent
Coming back into line with the Sun

Lunar eclipse
If a full moon moves into the Earth's shadow, it briefly turns orange.

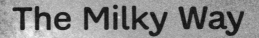

The Milky Way

We, and our Solar System, are part of a bigger area known as the Milky Way. You can see it as a pale, cloudy trail on clear nights or from high mountains. This view of it is seen from the top of Mauna Kea in Hawaii. The shapes below are big telescopes.

Home galaxy The Milky Way contains about 300 billion stars. It has two main spiral arms and several smaller ones sweeping out from a bar-shaped core. From the side, its shape looks like two fried eggs stuck together.

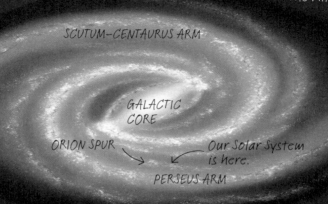

The Milky Way

SCUTUM–CENTAURUS ARM

GALACTIC CORE

ORION SPUR

Our Solar System is here.

PERSEUS ARM

* **Around we go** Just as Earth orbits the Sun, so the Sun and the Milky Way's other stars circle the galactic core at the heart of the Galaxy. Our Sun goes around the Galaxy once every 230 million years, and is on its 20th orbit.

* **Bright arms** Spiral galaxies like ours have arms because they have lots of hot, bright, young stars. These don't live long, so by the time they reach the edge of their arm, they've died.

MILKY WAY FACTS

Galaxy type: Barred spiral galaxy

Side view: ──────

Diameter: 100,000 light years

Age: 8 billion years

Thickness: (core) 12,000 light years   (arms) 1,000 light years

Distance from Sun to galactic core: 28,000 light years

Meteors and meteorites

This blazing streak, called a meteor or shooting star, is a piece of space rubble burning up in Earth's atmosphere.

Chunks of rock, metal and ice known as meteoroids circle the Sun. Some enter the Earth's atmosphere, where most burn up. When they're burning up, they're called meteors. The few that reach the Earth's surface are known as meteorites.

* **Meteorites** Most meteors are pea sized and vaporize in seconds, but each year, about 50,000 meteors heavier than 10g (0.4oz) land on the Earth. They are then called meteorites.

* **Meteor showers** Most nights, you might see 2 or 3 meteors an hour, but at times when Earth passes through a cloud of icy meteoroids, the rate soars into a 'meteor shower'. In the Perseid shower in August, up to 75 meteors an hour can be seen.

* **Tunguska** At 7:14 a.m. on June 30, 1908, what was probably a meteorite exploded over remote Tunguska in Russia, flattening trees over 2,150 sq km (830 sq miles). Five hours later, the Earth would have turned and it could have hit the city of St. Petersburg.

* **Sky watch** The *Pan-STARRS* telescope in Hawaii uses the world's largest digital camera to scan the skies for Tunguska-style dangers. Every minute, it takes two 1.4 gigapixel photos. If printed out, the photos would cover a basketball court.

Meteor Crater in Arizona, USA, is 1.2km (¾ mile) wide. It was made by a large meteorite 50,000 years ago.

MAJOR ANNUAL METEOR SHOWERS

Quadrantid: peaks January 4, comes from constellation Boötes

Perseid: peaks August 12, comes from constellation Perseus

Leonid: peaks November 17, comes from constellation Leo

Geminid: peaks December 13, comes from constellation Gemini

Solar sights

The Aurora Borealis (Northern Lights) is a vivid light show seen in the sky in far northern places. It happens when invisible particles from the Sun hit a magnetic force field around the Earth.

* **Circumhorizon arcs**
  These are dazzling, rainbow-like effects seen only when a very high summer Sun lights up wispy ice clouds. They are fragments of a giant ice halo (see below) along the horizon.

* **Ice haloes** Low sunlight shining through ice clouds can produce a ghostly halo around the Sun, sometimes with bright lights on either side, known as sundogs.

* **Daily illusions** When you see the setting Sun touch the horizon, it has already set. Its rays have to go through the atmosphere's light-bending gases before reaching you. They have further to go when the Sun is low in the sky, so they bend more, making it look higher than it is. This also gives us an early sunrise.

* **Lights out** A solar eclipse is a rare event when the Moon crosses the Sun's face, hiding its light from us. If the Moon is in the far part of its oval orbit, it looks smaller than the Sun, creating an 'annular eclipse'.

Annular eclipse, or 'ring of fire'

MORE SOLAR SIGHTS

Sun pillar: pillar of light seen above the Sun in icy conditions

Green flash: very rare green light seen above a sunrise or sunset

Glory: circular rainbow-like halo, often around your shadow

Brocken spectre: giant shadow seen in mountain mist, inside a 'glory'

Constellations

Since ancient times, people have played 'join the dots' with the stars, making up imaginary pictures called constellations. Many are named after mythical figures. This is Orion the Hunter. His belt of three bright stars is easy to spot.

* **Star names** The most brilliant stars usually have either an Arabic or a Greek name, plus an English name. The brightest star is Sirius, a name of Greek origin, but it's also known as the Dog Star.

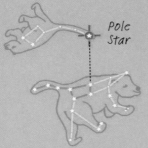

Pole Star

* **Polar Bear** The constellation Ursa Major, the Great Bear, contains another pattern (shown in orange) called the Plough or Big Dipper. Two of its stars point to the Pole Star, showing the way north.

* **Zodiac** This set of 12 constellations lines the path the Sun and planets seem to follow around the sky each year. At least half the patterns, such as Leo the Lion, were named as early as 1000BC, in Babylon.

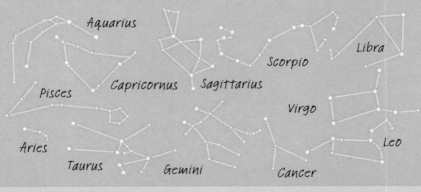

Aquarius
Scorpio
Libra
Capricornus Sagittarius
Pisces
Virgo
Aries
Leo
Taurus Gemini Cancer

CONSTELLATION FACTS

Named longest ago: Ursa Major

Brightest: Crux (Southern Cross)

Last to be named: Carina (Keel),

Faintest: Mensa (Table Mountain)

Puppis (Poop Deck), Vela (Sail)

Biggest: Hydra (Water Snake)

Most stars: Centaurus (Centaur)

Smallest: Crux (Southern Cross)

Fewest stars: Caelum (Chisel)

Orion

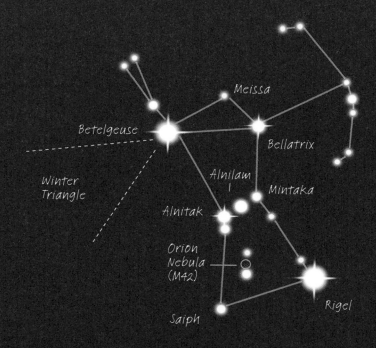

Meissa

Betelgeuse

Bellatrix

Winter
Triangle

Alnilam

Mintaka

Alnitak

Orion
Nebula
(M42)

Rigel

Saiph

Meaning:	The Hunter
Look for it:	North: winter; South: summer
Brightest star:	Rigel ("left foot")

Orion represents a giant hunter, with a dazzling,
gem-studded belt, and bright stars marking his broad
shoulders, foot and knee. These include bluish Rigel, the
seventh brightest star, and red Betelgeuse, the tenth
brightest. Orion holds a club, threatening Taurus the Bull
who, as the stars turn, backs away from him. His sword is
made of two stars and the Orion Nebula.

Taurus

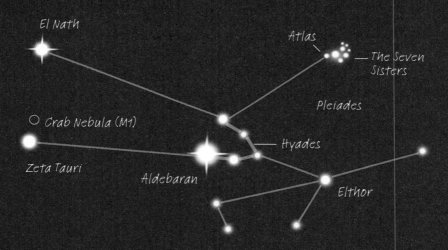

El Nath

Atlas

The Seven Sisters

Pleiades

Crab Nebula (M1)

Hyades

Zeta Tauri

Aldebaran

Elthor

Meaning:	The Bull
Look for it:	North: winter; South: summer
Brightest star:	Aldebaran ("the follower")

In a Greek myth, Zeus, king of the gods, turned into a bull
to carry off a princess across the sea. The Bull's shoulder
is marked by the Pleiades, a sparkling open cluster named
after the Seven Sisters, daughters of a giant named Atlas.
The Hyades (another cluster, named after their half-
sisters) and bright, reddish Aldebaran, make up the Bull's
head. The dim Crab Nebula is the remains of a supernova
(a massive star explosion) seen in 1054.

Perseus

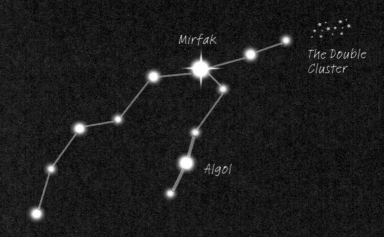

Mirfak

The Double Cluster

Algol

Meaning:	The Hero
Look for it:	North: autumn; South: spring
Brightest star:	Mirfak ("elbow")

Perseus was a hero in Greek mythology. He beheaded
a snake-haired demon, Medusa, whose gaze could
turn anything to stone. He cut off her head and used
it to rescue Princess Andromeda from a sea monster,
Cetus, changing it to stone. Algol ("the demon") is an
eclipsing variable star which represents Medusa's
head, carried by Perseus. Every 2.8 days, it dims to
a third of its brightness in just a few hours. Around
August 8th-14th each year, the Perseid meteor shower
appears in this part of the sky.

Cassiopeia

Meaning: The Queen

Look for it: North: all year

Brightest star: Schedar ("breast")

In Greek legends, Cassiopeia was the queen of Joppa
(now Jaffa in Israel), mother of Andromeda. She was
very vain and boasted that she and her daughter were
more beautiful than all the mermaids. This angered
Poseidon, the sea god, who sent a sea monster to attack
Joppa. This bright, zigzag constellation shows Cassiopeia
on her throne. For half of every night, as her stars turn
around, she has to cling on for dear life as her throne
tips upside-down.

March to May

Maps for the northern hemisphere

Best times to look:
March 15th at 11pm
April 15th at 9pm
May 15th at 10pm

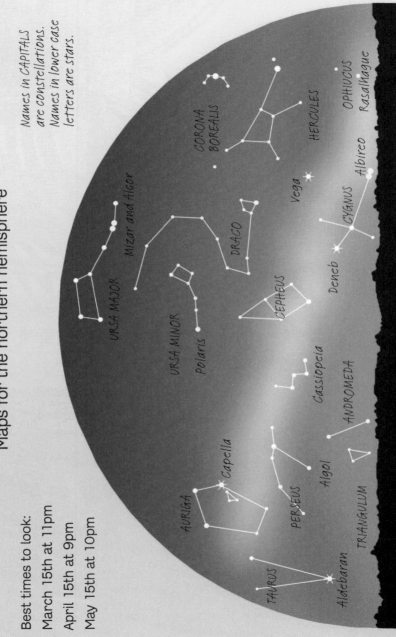

Names in CAPITALS are constellations. Names in lower case letters are stars.

West

Looking north

East

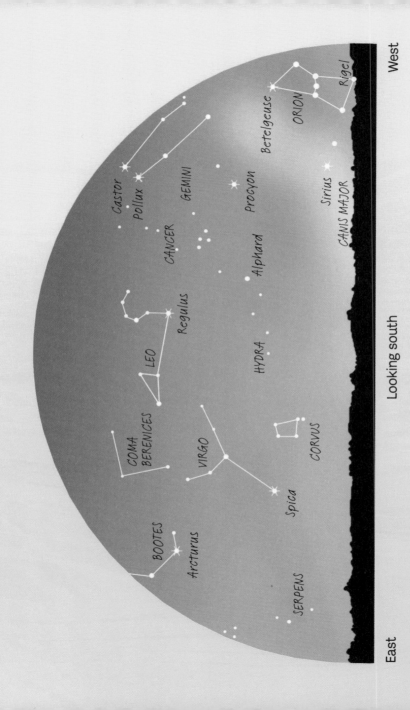

East

Looking south

West

17

March to May

Maps for the southern hemisphere

Best times to look:
March 15th at 11pm
April 15th at 10pm
May 15th at 8pm

West

Looking north

East

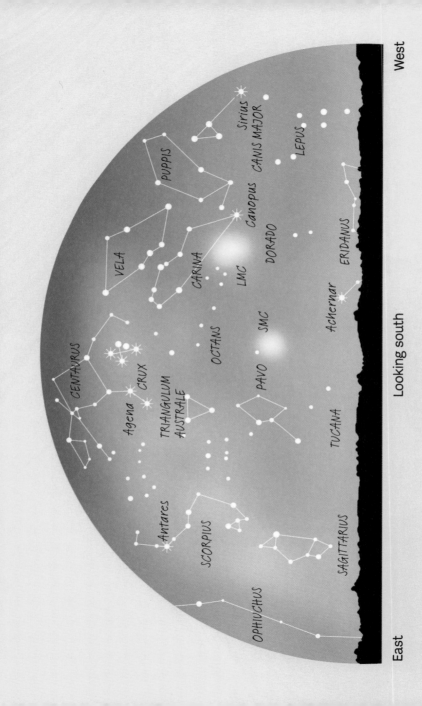

East

West

Looking south

19

June to August

Maps for the northern hemisphere

Best times to look:
June 15th at 2am
July 15th at midnight
August 15th at 10pm

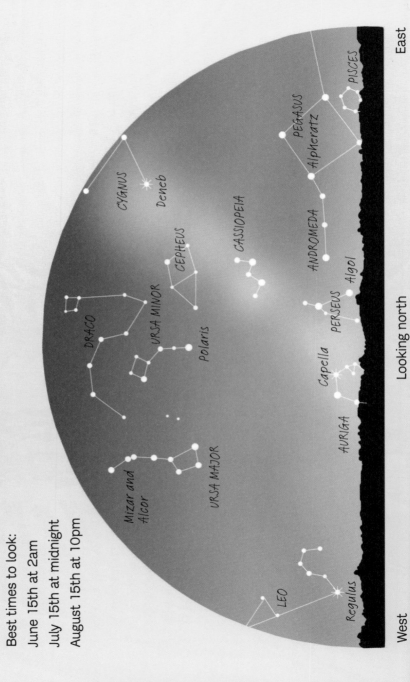

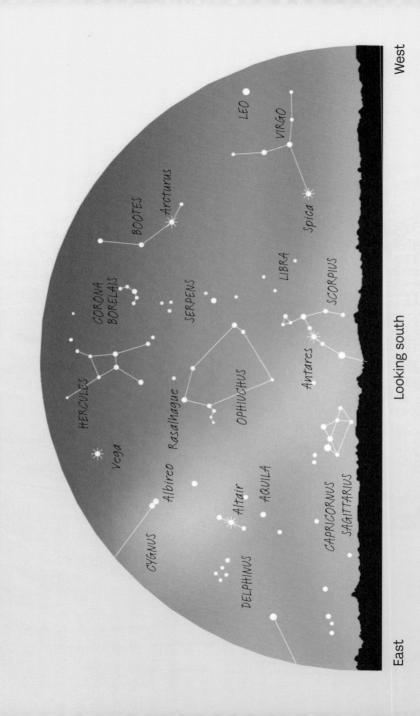

West

Looking south

East

LEO

VIRGO

Spica

Arcturus

BOOTES

LIBRA

SCORPIUS

Antares

SERPENS

CORONA
BORELAIS

OPHIUCHUS

Rasalhague

HERCULES

Vega

Albireo

Altair

AQUILA

CYGNUS

DELPHINUS

CAPRICORNUS

SAGITTARIUS

21

June to August

Maps for the southern hemisphere

Best times to look:
June 15th at midnight
July 15th at 10pm
August 15th at 8pm

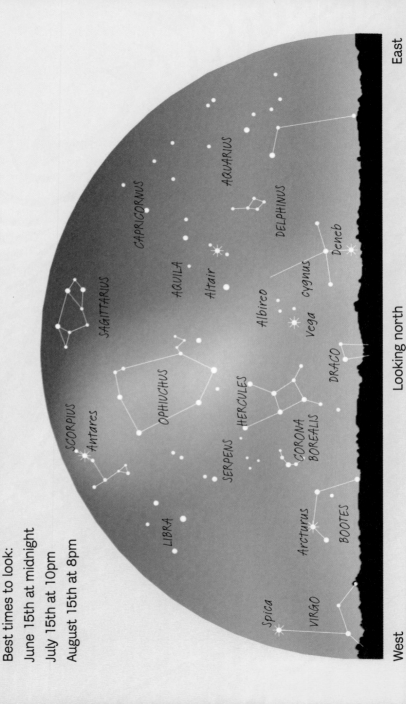

West

Looking north

East

East

West

Looking south

23

September to November

Maps for the northern hemisphere

Best times to look:
September 15th at 11pm
October 15th at 10pm
November 15th at 8pm

West

Looking north

East

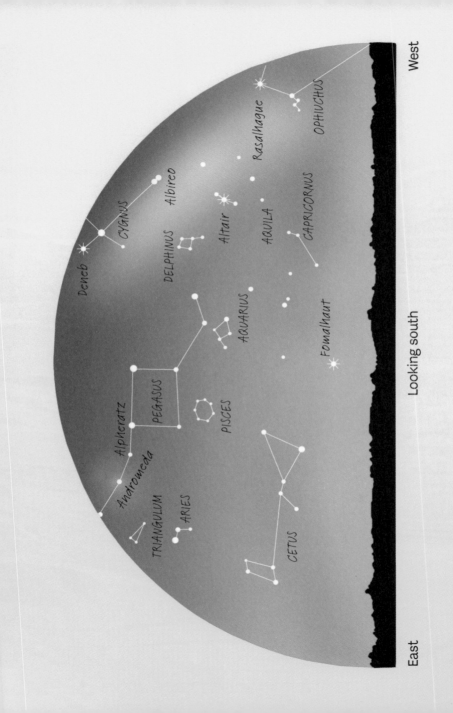

East

West

Looking south

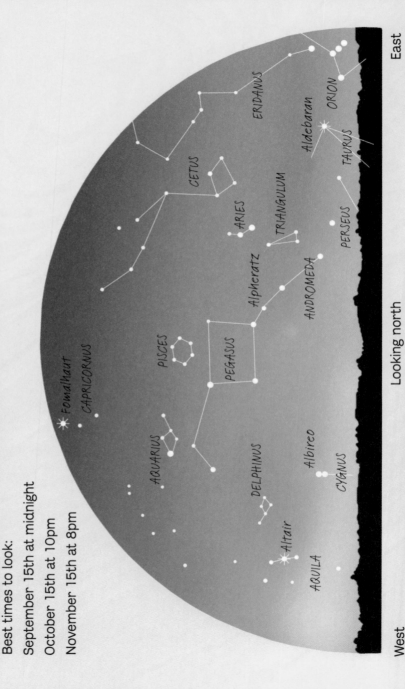

September to November

Maps for the southern hemisphere

Best times to look:
September 15th at midnight
October 15th at 10pm
November 15th at 8pm

West   Looking north   East

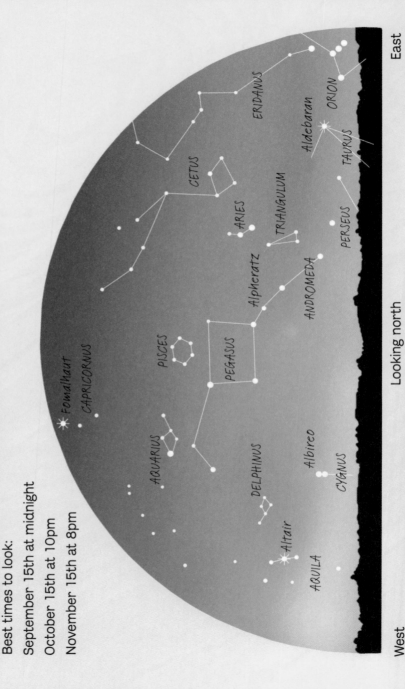

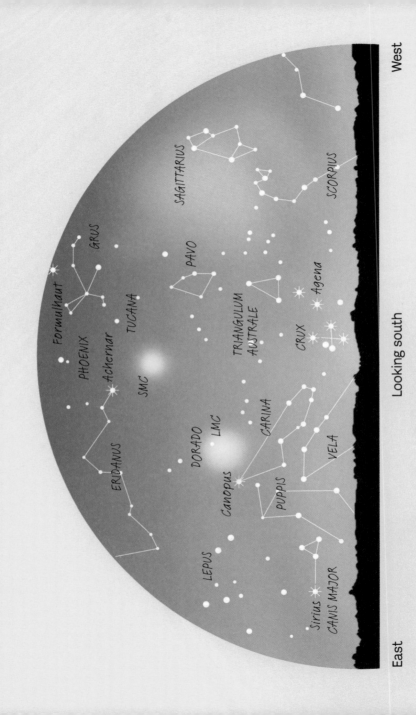

East

Looking south

West

December to February

Maps for the northern hemisphere

Best times to look:
December 15th at 11pm
January 15th at 9pm
February 15th at 7pm

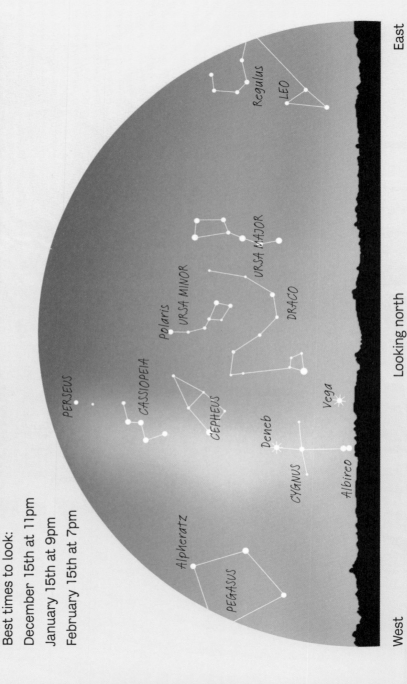

East

Looking south

West

December to February

Maps for the southern hemisphere

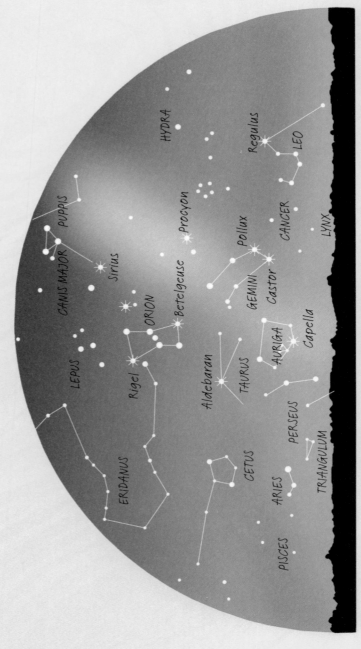